BRAIN GAMES™

Christmas
PICTURE PUZZLES

Publications International, Ltd.

Image Sources: Clipart, Dreamstime, iStock Photo, Jupiter Images Unlimited, Photodisc, Shutterstock

Contributing Writers: Holli Fort and Laura Pearson

Front cover puzzle: *Wrapped and Ready to Go*, see pages 54–55.
Back cover puzzle: *That Jolly Old Elf,* see page 70.

Louis Weber, CEO
Publications International, Ltd.
7373 North Cicero Avenue
Lincolnwood, Illinois 60712

ISBN-13: 978-1-4127-9808-2
ISBN-10: 1-4127-9808-6

Manufactured in China.

8 7 6 5 4 3 2 1

Celebrate a Season of Changes! ■ 4

Level 1 ■ 5

Start the season off right with these nice and easy puzzles.

Level 2 ■ 46

Look a little more carefully at these festive photos—they're getting tougher!

Level 3 ■ 87

These changes are more subtle, so keep alert in this deceptively sweet section.

Level 4 ■ 128

These puzzles may be twinkling, but they're the hardest of the bunch!

Answers ■ 169

Celebrate a Season of Changes!

Are you ready to test your powers of observation? Not only are the picture puzzles in this book cheerful and merry, they also challenge your mind. Just look carefully at the pictures on each page to see if you can spot the differences between them. But beware—the puzzles get progressively harder with each level! The number of changes increases, the differences become subtler, and the pictures are more densely detailed.

As you move through the book, you'll hone your observational skills. Keep in mind that we've altered each picture in a variety of ways. You might find the pattern on a beautifully wrapped present has changed, an ornament has been taken down, a shadow or reflection has been erased, or another gingerbread cookie has appeared on a platter. Remember, some puzzles demand that you pay extra attention, as the changes may be found in the smallest details.

Not all puzzles feature just two images. Some puzzles involve finding a single change among a grouping of three, four, or six of the same picture. You'll need to look carefully at all the photos to discover which one is not like the others.

You can check your work with the answer key located at the back of the book. The original picture is presented in black and white, with the changes circled and numbered.

Putting your brain to work and focusing your attention are great ways to find fun, enjoyment, and challenge during these busy days. So take a deep breath, clear your mind, and get ready to find all the differences in *Brain Games*™: *Christmas Picture Puzzles!*

Sleigh-t of Hand

'Tis the season for giving—and we've given you a real challenge with this puzzle!

Baking Basics

You'll have to be one tough cookie to find all of these changes!

Answers on page 169.

Ornamental Garden

We've sown quite a few changes into this puzzle. Can you reap them all?

Snowman on the Move

We're sure you'll roll right through this puzzle,
picking up all the changes along the way.

Answers on page 169.

Holiday Hearth Hunt

Warm up your brain as you scour the scene for changes.

4 changes

Tree Trimmers

Hang in there until you spot all of the differences in these ornament pictures.

Answers on page 169.

Jingle Boy

This adorable Santa is hiding something. Can you
find the single change in one of these pictures?

1

2

3

4

A Feast for the Eyes

We've spread out a buffet of changes for you to find, so please help yourself.

Answers on page 170.

Cozy Getaway

Retreat from life's daily stresses as you scan this
peaceful winter scene for changes.

Nutcracker Challenge

Crack this puzzle wide open by finding the changes between these pictures.

Dot Matrix

Don't go dotty trying to spot all of the changes in these pictures.

Answers on page 170.

Cookie Centerpiece Challenge

Take a nibble at this puzzle to see if you can detect the sweet notes of changes.

Gone Buggy

Try not to drive yourself buggy finding the changes
in this traditional winter scene.

Answers on page 171.

Sandy Claus

Take a look at these sandy Santas, and see if you
can dig up the single change among them.

1

2

3

4

5

6

Table for Two

The scene is set, and some changes have been folded
in for good measure. Can you spot them all?

Answers on page 171.

Candy Express

Set a course for delicious excitement as you search
for the changes in this candy-filled scene.

Tinted Teaser

No need to raise a *hue* and cry—just find all of the differences in these Christmas morning scenes.

Gift Exchange

We'd give you the answers to this puzzle, but we're
sure you'll have it all wrapped up in no time.

Answers on page 171.

A December to Remember

Cruise through this puzzle, and fill up your
mental tank by finding all of the differences.

Fit to Be Tied

Wrap up this puzzle by finding the single
change hidden among these gifts.

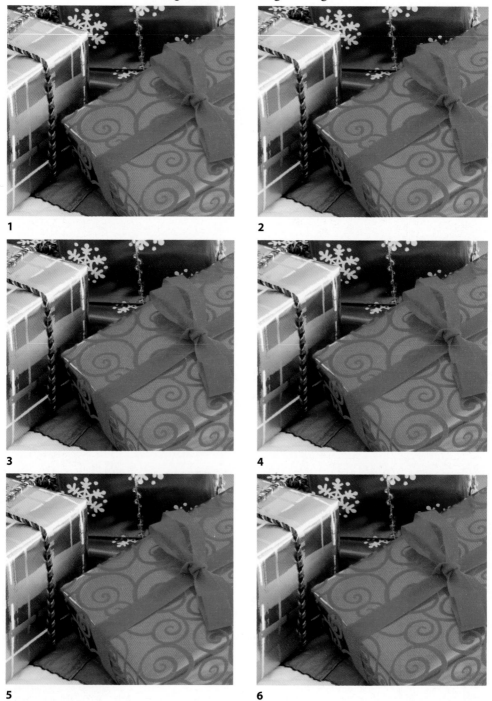

1

2

3

4

5

6

Answer on page 172.

Strange Benchfellows

These brothers put a snow day to excellent use—and so can
you, by spotting all of the differences in these pictures.

Boughs and Bows and Bears, Oh My!

We're sure you'll have a *bear*-y good time finding
all of the changes in these pictures.

Answers on page 172.

It's All in the Packaging

Tag the changes in these pictures to tie up the loose ends in this puzzle.

Basket Case
Don't pack it in—look for the changes we've made to this scene.

Unwrap the Fun

Peel away the layers to reveal all of the changes
in this Christmas morning scene.

Answers on page 173.

Gingerbread Guesser

Look, look, as fast as you can!
Can you catch all the changes in gingerbread land?

Christmas Morning Delight

You may be surprised and amazed when you unwrap
the single change among these photos.

1

2

3

4

Answer on page 173.

A Warm Welcome

Bask in the warm glow of the changes that can be found in this homey scene.

. . . by the Mantel with Care

Take stock(ing) of all the changes in these two Christmas Eve pictures.

Girl's Best Friend

Forget diamonds—on a snowy day, curling up with a canine friend is worth a million bucks! Can you sniff out the changes in this scene?

Gift Guesser

Turn it this way and that, shake it, do whatever you
have to do to unwrap the changes in this puzzle.

Altered Elves

Help these elves tally up the changes between pictures.

Answers on page 174.

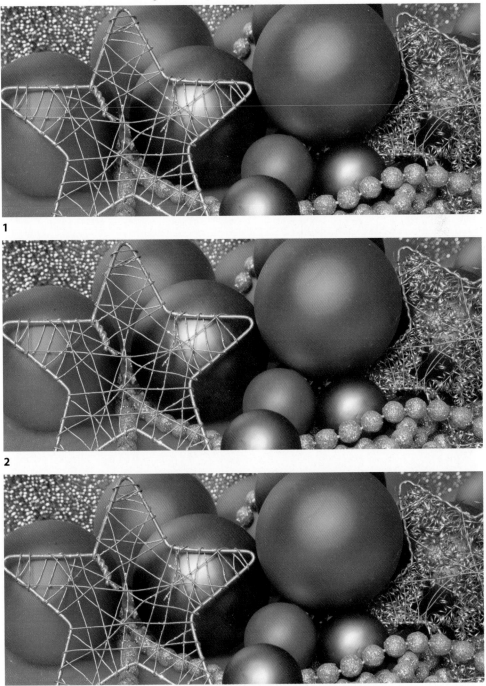

Star Search

You'll go down to the wire trying to find a single
change among these ornament photos.

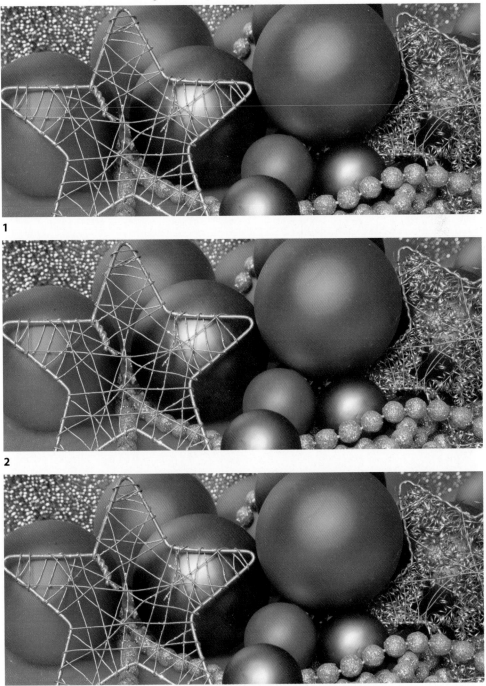

1

2

3

Packaged to Go
How quickly can you wrap up this puzzle by finding all of the changes?

That's the Way the Cookies Crumble
Whip up a batch of sweet changes to solve this puzzle!

Answers on page 174.

Santa's Helper Hunt

Can you track down every last change between these photos?

Cowboy Christmas

These photos were the same—then we steered one in another direction.

Answers on page 175.

Deck the Walls

One of these photos is wreathed in changes. How many can you find?

Gathering of Gifts

Search among these mini gift boxes and gingerbread
cookies to see if you can find the differences.

Answers on page 175.

Picture-Perfect Puzzle

Take a close look at this family photo, and you'll find the changes in a flash!

Hoppy Christmas!

Compare these pictures, and a single change should leap out at you.

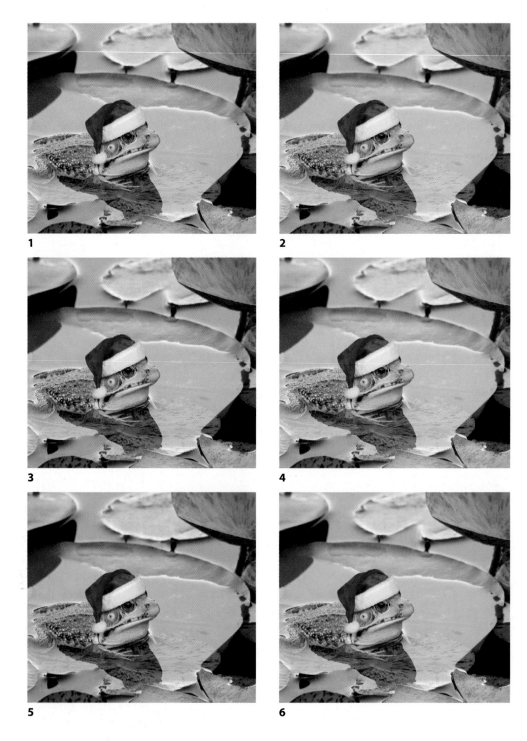

1

2

3

4

5

6

50

Answer on page 175.

Seasonal Sweets

We've made some modifications to this meal. Satisfy
your puzzle-solving appetite and find them all.

Christmas Cheer

Compare these jolly snowmen—and surrounding scenes—to find all the changes we've made.

Answers on page 176.

Santa Switch

These Russian Father Christmas dolls have undergone some fine handcrafting.
See if you can carve out a list of the changes.

Wrapped and Ready to Go

These presents are not quite ready to be handed out—first, you
need to give them your attention to find all of the changes.

Holiday Best

These well-dressed boys can't wait for dinner to be served.
Can you find all the ways we've dressed up this photo?

Cookie Exchange

Peruse this pretty tray, and see if you can find all the differences we've baked in.

Christmas Countdown

Ready for a challenge? Search for the ways we've transformed this picture.

Answers on page 176.

Homes for the Holidays

One of these pictures is housing a single change—can you hunt it down?

1

2

3

4

Enchanting Entry

This entryway is all decked out in Christmas reds and greens.
See if you can find the changes flowering in one of these photos.

Answers on page 177.

Sledding Switcheroo

Make tracks in a race to the finish as you search for all
of the changes between these two sledding scenes.

Glowing Gifts

Your present task: Browse these boxes, bells, boughs, and bows for differences.

Answers on page 177.

Cactus Choir

These desert-dwelling Santas are awfully cute.
Can you tune in to the differences we've made?

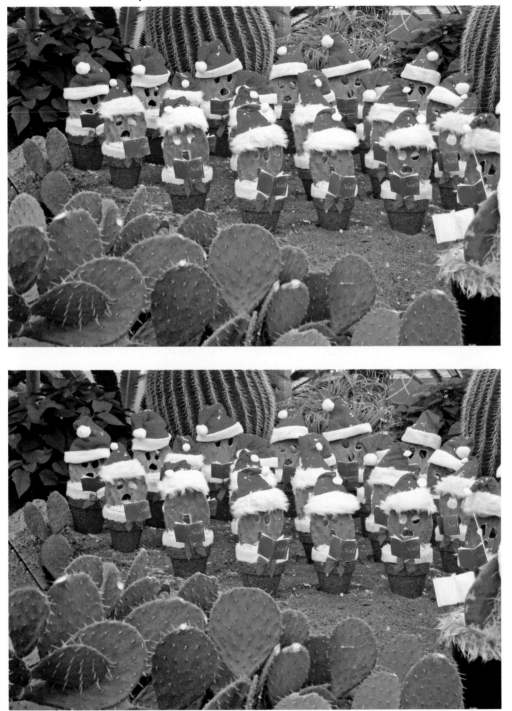

Now Presenting . . .

. . . a puzzle for you! (We hope it's not too much of a handful.)

Answers on page 177.

Holiday Magic

One of these serene scenes displays some differences. Take a close look.

Answers on page 178.

Special Delivery

This gang comes bearing gifts; these photos come bearing differences. Look carefully.

Browse the Boughs...

...and see if you can find a single change tucked into one of these pictures.

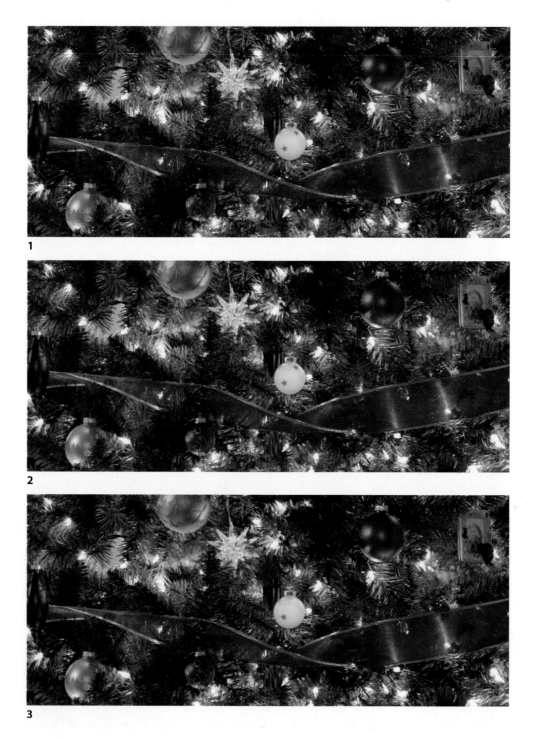

1

2

3

Answer on page 178.

Frosty Habitat

Chill out as you search this icy landscape for changes.

That Jolly Old Elf

It would be a real treat if you could find all the ways we've altered this picture.

Answers on page 178.

Treasures Beneath the Tree

One of these photos is not like the other. Can you bear to find all the differences?

Candyland Caper

It would be a sweet treat to find all of the differences in
these delectable scenes. Can't you just taste victory?

'Tis the Season . . .

. . . for festive table settings. Pull up a chair,
and see if you can locate all the changes.

Answers on page 179.

"Snow Place Like Home"

These photos were the same, but then the changes snowballed. Can you find them all?

Night Lights

Examine these peaceful nighttime scenes for a single change.

1

2

3

4

5

6

Answer on page 179.

Pile of Presents

Look carefully at these pretty packages to see how they differ.

Christmas Surprise

This little girl couldn't be more pleased with her purple puppy,
and we'd be pleased if you found all of the differences!

Santa's Helpers

These holiday helpers have done the wrapping; solving the puzzle is up to you!

Answers on page 180.

Night Before Christmas

Uh-oh . . . a creature is stirring! She wants to find
what Santa left behind; can you find the changes?

Gift Swap

These photos don't offer an even exchange—there are quite a few differences. Explore your gift for observation and find them all.

Answers on page 180.

Season's Eatings

Dinner is served! Can you find a single difference in one of these holiday meals?

1

2

3

4

Answer on page 180.

That's a Wrap!

This picture puzzle shouldn't pose too much of a challenge—just look carefully.

Let It Snow

By now you've had plenty of training. You know how to find the differences!

Answers on page 180.

The Light Brigade

We're sure you'll charge right through this puzzle in search of changes.

Gifts Galore

Put your gifts of observation to the test as you
search for changes in these pictures.

Answers on page 181.

Better to Light a Candle . . .

No one will be able to hold a candle to you after
you find all of the changes in this puzzle!

Snowscape Search

This snowstorm has brought something extra—a
single change lurking among the pictures.

1

2

3

4

5

6

Answer on page 181.

White and Red All Over

This all-white decor has been enlivened for the holidays.
Get into the spirit of the season as you hunt for changes.

Wreathed in Changes

There's been a steep increase in changes to this puzzle. Can you spot them all?

Answers on page 181.

Smart Cookies

Look, look as fast as you can to find all the changes in this gingerbread span.

Some Assembly Required

Can you put together a complete list of the differences between these scenes?

In the Toy Department

Holiday shopping is sometimes a chore, but it will be pure pleasure
to fill your basket with the changes between these photos.

Answers on page 182.

Cap It Off with a Puzzle

This puzzle makes a great topper for any holiday!

Ornamental Outlook
We've made one purely decorative change to
one of these photos. Can you find it?

1

2

3

Answer on page 182.

Manger Mystery

Can you find all of the differences in these nativity scenes?

Ceramics Class

How long do you "figure" it will take you to spot
all of the changes among these figurines?

Answers on page 183.

On the Antlers of a Dilemma

This family scene has definitely evolved! Can you spot all of the changes?

Puzzling Packages

Make your list (of changes) and check it twice
to make sure you've covered everything.

An Old-Fashioned Christmas

Take a trip down memory lane while searching
for changes in these nostalgic photos.

The Light Fantastic

Shed a bright light on these photos to find
the single change lurking in one of them.

1

2

3

4

Sale-a-brate!

One look and you'll be sold on finding all
of the changes in these shopping scenes.

Answers on page 183.

Step Up to the Plate

You'll hit a home run by finding all of the differences between these photos.

Trial by Fire

Make your best case for finding all of the differences in these fireside photos.

Wrap It Up

You've got a box seat to the changes offered in this puzzle!

Answers on page 184.

Waterfront Light Show

Reflect closely on these pictures to see if all of the changes come to the surface.

Gift Bagged

Don't be left holding the (gift) bag! Find all
of the differences between these pictures.

Answers on page 184.

A Snowy Ride

You'll be tempted to take this puzzle at a gallop, but if you slow down to a walk and take off your blinders, you'll find the single change hiding in these photos.

1

2

3

4

5

6

Answer on page 184.

Holiday Village Stumper

There's nothing miniature about the number of changes you'll need to find in these pictures in order to solve the puzzle.

Answers on page 185.

Not a Creature Was Stirring…

…not even a mouse. They were all quietly stocking up
on all of the changes in these fireside scenes.

All Spruced Up

It may take you all 12 days of Christmas to find some
of the sneaky changes hidden in this puzzle!

Answers on page 185.

8 changes

One-Stop Shopping

Fill up your remaining shopping-day downtime with this challenging puzzle.

Answers on page 185.

Just Desserts

This puzzle makes a perfect finish to a holiday celebration of changes.

Zen and Now

These peaceful scenes are harboring one single change. Can you find it?

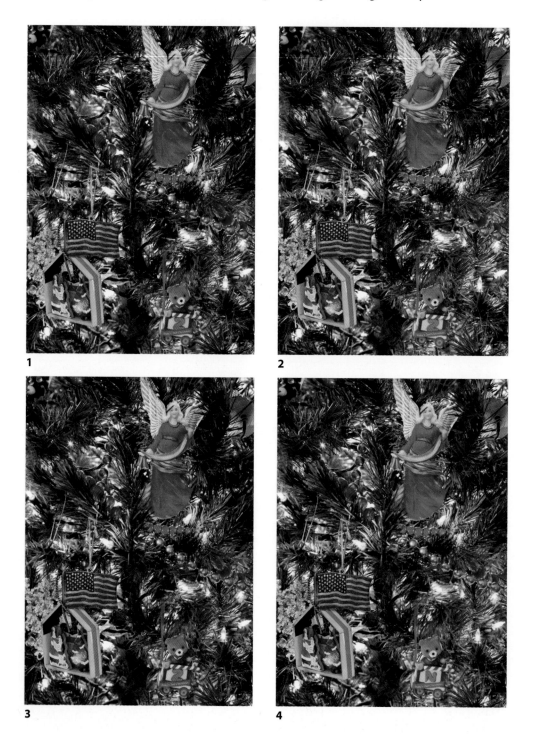

1

2

3

4

Answer on page 185.

Let There Be Light

Can you shed some light on the changes between pictures?

Secret Santa

We've made some changes to this gift exchange. Can you spot them all?

Answers on page 186.

Alpine High

This isn't the bunny slope—solving this puzzle will take concentration and skill. Just find all of the changes between pictures.

Chocolate Challenge
This puzzle is a sweet treat for the eyes.

Answers on page 186.

Fire Drill

How quickly can you determine the extent
of the changes between these pictures?

Answers on page 186.

Alley Oops

A quick stroll through this puzzle should reveal some of the changes,
but to find them all, a more thoughtful meander is required.

Answers on page 186.

Noel, Noel
These Christmas arrangements contain
some differences. How many can you find?

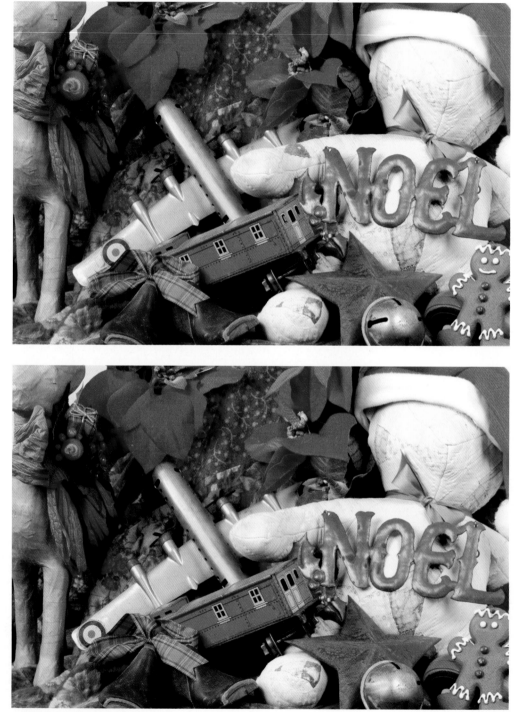

Answers on page 187.

Group of Gifts

Scan these festively wrapped presents for some decorative differences.

Snowed In

This mountain village is covered in snow. Can you dig out the differences?

Answers on page 187.

Christmas Cluster

Search among the fruit, trinkets, coffee, and nuts to discover a single change.

1

2

3

4

Gingerbread Neighborhood
Compare these candy-coated scenes to find the differences.

Answers on page 187.

Cozy Kids

We've blanketed this photo in changes. How many can you uncover?

Lights of London

Inspect this illuminated cathedral and Christmas tree,
and you will find some landmark changes.

Doll-Making Workshop

Deck the dolls with hats and ribbons! When you're done,
study this workspace for the changes we've made.

Answers on page 188.

Interior Decorating

Hope you can make room for another challenge:
Study this pristine scene, and find all the differences.

Now, Dasher! Now, Dancer!

Even reindeer need a snack now and then! Feed your mental
hunger by seeking out all of the delicious changes in these scenes.

Perplexing Place Setting

Everything was in place, but then we set up a challenge
for you and made just one change. Can you find it?

1

2

3

4

5

6

Mind the Store

This department store is crammed with holiday items.
We've tossed in some changes, too. Can you find them?

Answers on page 188.

See the Light

When it comes to holiday decorating, this household went all out!
The differences aren't glaringly obvious, so look carefully.

The Christmas Story

While this family was having story time,
we plotted a few changes. Can you find them?

Answers on page 189.

Nutcrackers Old and New
Get cracking to find the changes in these two photos.

Answers on page 189.

Cookie-Cutter Challenge

10 changes

Don't *dessert* a challenge like this: Look carefully
at these confections and find what's different.

Jingle Bell Jumble

By now, this type of puzzle should definitely ring a bell.
Look closely—you know what to do!

Answers on page 189.

Skating Rink Riddler

Watch out for thin ice as you find the changes in these skating scenes.

Ornamentally Yours

Inspect these ornaments carefully as you search
for the single change in these photos.

1

2

3

Answer on page 190.

Christmas Village

Examine these glittering holiday houses, and figure out what changed.

Tree Trimming Teaser

We know you can find all of the changes *elf* you look hard enough.

Oh, Holy Night

Compare these illuminated buildings, and the differences will come to light.

Answers on page 190.

The Present Predicament

It's not quite time to open presents, but it *is* time
to open your eyes to this challenge!

Trays of Treats

Survey these sweets, and see if you can sniff out the changes.

Answers on page 190.

Poinsettia Puzzle

We've planted a single change in one of these photos. Search carefully.

1

2

3

4

5

6

Answer on page 191.

155

Window-Shopping Wonderland

Enjoy browsing the offerings, because we think you'll find
the selection in these photos very… illuminating.

Answers on page 191.

Christmas Eve Challenge

"The stockings were hung by the chimney with care…"
That is, until we made some alterations!

LEVEL 4

10 changes

No Time Like the Present . . .

. . . to hunt for all the changes we've made.
We wouldn't want to keep them under wraps!

Answers on page 191.

Snowy Street Scene

A chill is not all that's in the air in these pictures!
See how many differences you can find.

 Answers on page 191.

Family Gathering

By now you've gathered that these photos are not the same. That should be *grand*-ly ap-*parent*.

Beads, Bags, and Baubles

Try locating the differences between these photos. *Yule* be glad you did!

Answers on page 192.

Nativity Activity

We think you're stable enough to solve this one:
Look among the figurines and find a single change.

1

2

3

Answer on page 192.

Transformed Table

These photos were the same, but now the tables have turned.
Can you find all the changes we've made?

So Many Snowmen and Santas . . .

... and so many changes! Think you can find them all?

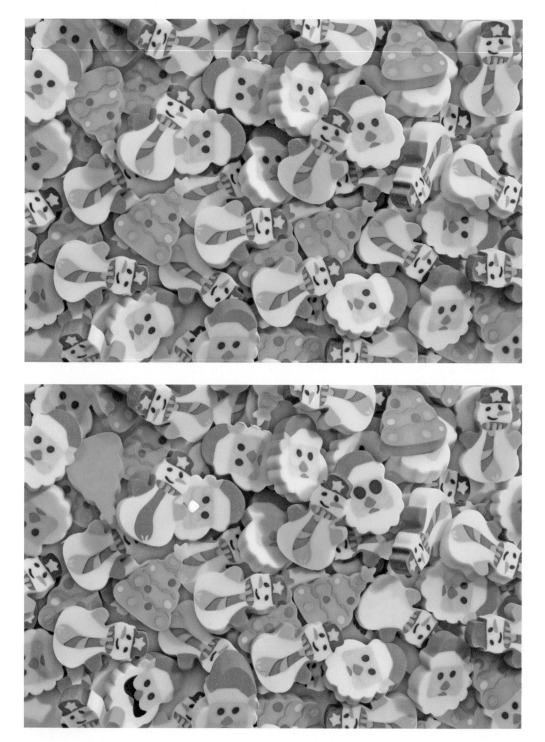

Answers on page 192.

Winterlude Challenge

Ottawa's Winterlude Festival is alive with changes. Can you spot them all?

Answers on page 192.

Snow-covered Cabins

One of these wintry scenes is not like the other.

Wood you be up for finding the differences?

Answers on page 192.

LEVEL 1

■ _Sleigh_-t of Hand, _(page 5)_ **1.** Red bell added; **2.** curtain lengthened; **3.** rope missing; **4.** gift added—someone's been good!; **5.** bow moved up and red bell gone.

■ Snowman on the Move, _(page 8)_ **1.** Carrot nose lengthened—snowman lied?; **2.** yellow handle turned blue; **3.** foot smaller; **4.** red wristband changed to black.

■ Baking Basics, _(page 6)_ **1.** Finger lengthened; **2.** apron straps turned solid red; **3.** heart deleted; **4.** side of apron turned pink.

■ Holiday Hearth Hunt, _(page 9)_ **1.** Ornament missing; **2.** green light turned red; **3.** white grout line deleted; **4.** Santa added; **5.** light switch rotated.

■ Ornamental Garden, _(page 7)_ **1.** Pointed ornament became round; **2.** orange and red balls switched; **3.** hook lengthened; **4.** gold top removed; **5.** red bead added.

■ Tree Trimmers, _(page 10)_ **1.** Gold scarf turned red; **2.** red stripe removed; **3.** scarf lengthened—it's cold on the tree!; **4.** rosy cheek added.

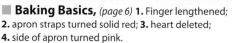

■ Jingle Boy, *(page 11)* **1.** Bell removed in photo 2.

■ Nutcracker Challenge, *(pages 14–15)* **1.** Blue stripe made red; **2.** stars removed; **3.** green gem added; **4.** green wheel turned red; **5.** bottom of staff removed.

■ A Feast for the Eyes, *(page 12)* **1.** Red berry added; **2.** wine glass filled up; **3.** yellow vegetable turned green; **4.** leaf removed; **5.** inside of pitcher turned tan.

■ Dot Matrix, *(page 16)* **1.** Side of heart squared off; **2.** red and blue dots switched; **3.** hand removed; **4.** dotted strip added; **5.** shirt turned black.

■ Cozy Getaway, *(page 13)* **1.** Cloud extended; **2.** window post removed; **3.** window on its side; **4.** boxes restacked; **5.** green trim turned red.

■ Cookie Centerpiece Challenge, *(page 17)* **1.** Flame extinguished; **2.** branch extended; **3.** white area turned red; **4.** red sprinkle eaten; **5.** branch trimmed.

Gone Buggy, *(page 18)* **1.** Light turned off; **2.** row of gold circles added; **3.** wheel missing; **4.** hat turned white from snowfall.

Candy Express, *(page 21)* **1.** Dark blue rectangle extended; **2.** yellow circle now blue; **3.** circle missing; **4.** green spiral turned yellow; **5.** circle became a square.

Sandy Claus, *(page 19)* **1.** Stick "button" added in photo 3.

Tinted Teaser, *(pages 22–23)* **1.** Purple ribbon turned hot pink; **2.** strap missing; **3.** socks pulled up to knees; **4.** white cuff gone.

Table for Two, *(page 20)* **1.** Napkin lost its point; **2.** flame shortened; **3.** red ribbon removed; **4.** glass taller.

Gift Exchange, *(page 24)* **1.** Bow smaller; **2.** gift given away; **3.** box lid turned gold; **4.** cord missing.

A December to Remember, *(page 25)*
1. White sign turned black; **2.** steering wheel made red;
3. red bow changed to white; **4.** white sign taken down.

Boughs and Bows and Bears, Oh My!,
(page 28) **1.** Branch blackened; **2.** pinecone added;
3. snowflake drifted to right side of hat; **4.** nose turned red from cold.

Fit to Be Tied, *(page 26)* **1.** White stripe deleted in photo 6.

It's All in the Packaging, *(page 29)* **1.** Green stripe turned red; **2.** spool end turned black; **3.** circles design replaced with vee; **4.** pen missing; **5.** ribbon deleted.

Strange Benchfellows, *(page 27)* **1.** Extra tree planted; **2.** stick added; **3.** bench post widened;
4. snowman's arm grew; **5.** white stripe gone.

Basket Case,
(pages 30–31)
1. Tail of ribbon disappeared;
2. red berries added;
3. pattern changed;
4. cinnamon stick lengthened;
5. red ribbon added.

■ **Unwrap the Fun,** *(page 32)* **1.** Star removed; **2.** gray pants turned black; **3.** lamp base upside-down; **4.** red ribbon turned white; **5.** ornament added.

■ **A Warm Welcome,** *(page 35)* **1.** White lights added; **2.** black pane line added; **3.** candle removed; **4.** curtain border straightened; **5.** plant grew.

■ **Gingerbread Guesser,** *(page 33)* **1.** Smile changed to O of surprise; **2.** candy puffed out; **3.** yellow gumdrop turned green; **4.** frosting line added; **5.** candy ornament hung.

■ **. . . by the Mantel with Care,** *(pages 36–37)* **1.** Black dot missing; **2.** candle blown out; **3.** design upside-down; **4.** green cracker added; **5.** stocking hung backward.

■ **Christmas Morning Delight,** *(page 34)* **1.** Toenails painted pink in photo 3.

■ **Girl's Best Friend,** *(page 38)* **1.** Yellow dot turned red; **2.** tree trimmed; **3.** windows connected; **4.** white car turned black; **5.** stars and writing erased.

Gift Guesser, *(page 39)* **1.** Yellow flower plucked; **2.** blue ribbon extended; **3.** red lightbulb removed; **4.** dead flower brought back to life—a Christmas miracle!; **5.** crack filled in.

Altered Elves, *(page 40)* **1.** Ribbon cut and discarded; **2.** hair gone; **3.** red stripe turned white; **4.** elf got a haircut.

Star Search, *(page 41)* **1.** Gold wire deleted in photo 2.

Packaged to Go, *(pages 42–43)* **1.** Earring missing; **2.** flower design erased; **3.** ribbon shifted to the right; **4.** leaf enlarged.

That's the Way the Cookies Crumble, *(page 44)* **1.** White frosting line erased; **2.** chocolate line added; **3.** white truffle replaced with brown; **4.** nut picked off.

Santa's Helper Hunt, *(page 45)* **1.** Santa missing; **2.** bow removed; **3.** snowman flipped; **4.** turtleneck extended—for increased neck warmth; **5.** light burned out.

LEVEL 2

■ **Cowboy Christmas,** *(page 46)* **1.** Red light bigger and brighter; **2.** red flowers appeared; **3.** cowboy hat turned brown; **4.** candlestick moved left; **5.** fire grew; **6.** fireplace poker moved right.

■ **Picture-Perfect Puzzle,** *(page 49)* **1.** Blue stripe added; **2.** ornament moved up and left; **3.** shirt sleeve longer; **4.** coil of ribbon added; **5.** T-shirt neck trim turned black; **6.** ornament lowered; **7.** section of hair grew.

■ **Deck the Walls,** *(page 47)* **1.** Bow added; **2.** wreaths switched places; **3.** bow turned gold; **4.** knob moved up; **5.** another wreath appeared; **6.** white wreath now solid green.

■ **Hoppy Christmas!,** *(page 50)* **1.** Lily pad changed in photo 5.

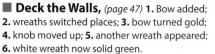

■ **Gathering of Gifts,** *(page 48)* **1.** Gold designs appeared; **2.** red bar added; **3.** gold stripe deleted; **4.** gold ribbon added; **5.** yellow buttons turned green; **6.** words erased.

■ **Seasonal Sweets,** *(page 51)* **1.** Place mat bigger; **2.** berry appeared; **3.** chair taken away; **4.** holly berry added; **5.** holly berries picked and eaten; **6.** another berry added.

■ **Christmas Cheer,** *(page 52)* **1.** Letter R flipped backward; **2.** signpost turned solid red; **3.** eyes spread apart; **4.** entryway filled in; **5.** CHRISTMAS deleted; **6.** hat turned blue.

■ **Holiday Best,** *(page 56)* **1.** Curtain extended; **2.** glass appeared; **3.** tie became red; **4.** crossbar added to window; **5.** designs on drawer painted over; **6.** lamp rod changed shape.

■ **Santa Switch,** *(page 53)* **1.** Staff top made oval; **2.** doll frowning; **3.** robe section missing; **4.** mittens swapped; **5.** foot disappeared under robe; **6.** nose missing.

■ **Cookie Exchange,** *(page 57)* **1.** Walnut moved up; **2.** gold bell added; **3.** orange center filled in; **4.** chocolate center bigger—yum!; **5.** more chocolate added here, too; **6.** heart-shape cookie appeared; **7.** hazelnut added.

■ **Wrapped and Ready to Go,** *(pages 54–55)* **1.** Gold stripe removed; **2.** snowman right side up; **3.** letters missing; **4.** green ribbon turned blue; **5.** white dots erased; **6.** extra red ribbon; **7.** white dot turned black.

■ **Christmas Countdown,** *(page 58)* **1.** Star bigger; **2.** gold ball turned red; **3.** gold star deleted; **4.** gold tinsel added; **5.** Sunday and Monday switched places; **6.** 2008 became 2007; **7.** gold star added.

■ **Homes for the Holidays,** *(page 59)* **1.** Post removed in photo 2.

■ **Glowing Gifts,** *(page 62)* **1.** Bow added; **2.** gift tag removed; **3.** ornament hung; **4.** votive appeared; **5.** coil of ribbon added; **6.** candle erased; **7.** ribbons added to box.

■ **Enchanting Entry,** *(page 60)* **1.** Design added to shutter; **2.** lantern moved up; **3.** stem thicker; **4.** white flowers grew; **5.** window filled in; **6.** shutters raised.

■ **Cactus Choir,** *(page 63)* **1.** Cactus leaf trimmed; **2.** eyes closed; **3.** mouth filled in; **4.** cactus leaf appeared; **5.** pom-pom fell off; **6.** book turned red.

■ **Sledding Switcheroo,** *(page 61)* **1.** Ski pole moved right; **2.** scarf missing—presumed blown away; **3.** rope turned black; **4.** sled rail uncovered; **5.** loop widened; **6.** rail extended.

■ **Now Presenting . . . ,** *(pages 64–65)* **1.** Gold cord deleted; **2.** package appeared; **3.** white stripe turned black; **4.** button added; **5.** present turned blue; **6.** present now green.

■ **Holiday Magic,** *(page 66)* **1.** Frame taken off wall; **2.** glass removed; **3.** apple added; **4.** green liquid added; **5.** picture moved down; **6.** picture hung up.

■ **Frosty Habitat,** *(page 69)* **1.** Penguin's nose missing; **2.** green ribbon made red; **3.** gold ornament added; **4.** branch grew; **5.** green border turned gold; **6.** zigzag wall smoothed out.

■ **Special Delivery,** *(page 67)* **1.** Taillight all red; **2.** square became solid green; **3.** tree moved left; **4.** bow turned gold; **5.** another bow appeared; **6.** pom-pom turned red.

■ **That Jolly Old Elf,** *(page 70)* **1.** Pom-pom smaller; **2.** red sleeve longer—will he be colder with less fur?; **3.** package now red; **4.** star cookie turned green; **5.** horizontal bar added; **6.** extra present—she must have been very good this year.

■ **Browse the Boughs . . . ,** *(page 68)* **1.** Star deleted in photo 3.

■ **Treasures Beneath the Tree,** *(page 71)* **1.** Block turned green; **2.** block became blue; **3.** silver ornament appeared; **4.** candy cane deleted—did the bear eat it?; **5.** top of yo-yo turned solid red; **6.** bird moved down.

Candyland Caper, *(pages 72–73)* **1.** Candy cane extended; **2.** purple candy added; **3.** fence section filled in; **4.** button fell off; **5.** candy upside-down; **6.** gingerbread woman smiling; **7.** candy cane eaten.

Night Lights, *(page 76)* **1.** Chimney disappeared in photo 4.

Pile of Presents, *(page 77)* **1.** Present and stockings switched places; **2.** leaves deleted; **3.** ornament moved left; **4.** more grapes appeared; **5.** branch longer; **6.** candy cane turned green; **7.** holly sprig upside-down.

'Tis the Season . . . , *(page 74)* **1.** White stripe deleted; **2.** bowl and plate switched places with cup; **3.** light fixture added; **4.** column deleted—hope it wasn't load-bearing!; **5.** bauble added to glass; **6.** fork appeared; **7.** tree taller.

Christmas Surprise, *(pages 78–79)* **1.** Wreath moved left; **2.** puppy closed his eye; **3.** silver ribbon snipped and discarded; **4.** ornament hung up; **5.** bow turned gold; **6.** box became green.

"*Snow* Place Like Home", *(page 75)* **1.** Snowman lost his nose; **2.** button added; **3.** mail slot closed up; **4.** snowman's arm removed; **5.** window crossbar erased; **6.** shrub bigger.

■ **Santa's Helpers,** *(page 80)* **1.** Leaf deleted; **2.** stripe became solid red; **3.** bow now red; **4.** blue bow appeared; **5.** fingers disappeared; **6.** side of bag became solid blue; **7.** bag handle turned red.

■ **Night Before Christmas,** *(page 81)* **1.** Ornament turned gold; **2.** ornament removed; **3.** poinsettia trimmed; **4.** stocking became green; **5.** fur trim now red; **6.** fire extinguished.

■ **Gift Swap,** *(page 82)* **1.** Red ornament turned gold; **2.** picture moved left; **3.** bracelets added—a recent gift?; **4.** ribbon extended; **5.** stripes deleted; **6.** V-neck became crewneck.

■ **Season's Eatings,** *(page 83)* **1.** Cherry tomato eaten in photo 3.

■ **That's a Wrap!,** *(pages 84–85)* **1.** Gold ribbon appeared; **2.** pom-pom deleted; **3.** gold bow bigger; **4.** square became solid gold; **5.** gold wrapping paper larger; **6.** red bow appeared.

■ **Let It Snow,** *(page 86)* **1.** SN written on board; **2.** gold ball added; **3.** bird flew away; **4.** windows closed; **5.** gold star deleted; **6.** Christmas tree turned right side up.

LEVEL 3

■ The Light Brigade, *(page 87)* **1.** Lights extended; **2.** porch railing taller; **3.** angled bar added to window; **4.** light rectangle darkened; **5.** grate strip deleted; **6.** light strand added; **7.** dark band added to post; **8.** green light illuminated.

■ Gifts Galore, *(page 88)* **1.** Star lowered; **2.** gold bow removed; **3.** bell deleted; **4.** leaf erased; **5.** angle of ribbon changed—someone was trying to peek!; **6.** gold tinsel added; **7.** leaf trimmed; **8.** ribbon widened.

■ Better to Light a Candle . . . , *(page 89)* **1.** Ruffle extended; **2.** hair now covering ear; **3.** brown cuff gone; **4.** necklace added—a gift from Santa?; **5.** button moved left; **6.** candle taller; **7.** white fabric turned gray; **8.** apple added; **9.** bow became vertical.

■ Snowscape Search, *(page 90)* **1.** Tree missing in photo 3.

■ White and Red All Over, *(page 91)* **1.** Lamp taller; **2.** red ribbons turned white—to better coordinate with the room?; **3.** white slipcover extended; **4.** handle removed; **5.** star taken down; **6.** pillow moved left; **7.** striped box added; **8.** lamp seam erased; **9.** table leg extended.

■ Wreathed in Changes, *(page 92)* **1.** Wreath extended upward; **2.** crack filled in; **3.** gray block turned black; **4.** gray block rotated; **5.** gray blocks added; **6.** flag straightened; **7.** triangle became an arch; **8.** black pants turned white.

ANSWERS

Smart Cookies, *(page 93)* **1.** Wing moved down; **2.** cookie flipped—star is shooting to right; **3.** design removed; **4.** frosting added to hole; **5.** windows connected; **6.** white X added; **7.** staff removed; **8.** bell bottom eaten—someone snuck a bite!

Cap It Off with a Puzzle, *(page 97)* **1.** Red ornament removed; **2.** green ribbon turned white; **3.** branch extended; **4.** dark blue ribbon added; **5.** branches pruned; **6.** bow deleted; **7.** yellow bottle removed; **8.** cord extended; **9.** leaf added.

Some Assembly Required, *(pages 94–95)* **1.** Shade lowered; **2.** belt loop added; **3.** black part under wheel removed; **4.** Santa upside-down; **5.** candy cane eaten; **6.** beads taken down—but Christmas isn't over!; **7.** sideburn lengthened; **8.** yellow screwdriver handle turned orange.

Ornamental Outlook, *(page 98)* **1.** Hook removed in photo 1.

Manger Mystery, *(page 99)* **1.** Light burned out; **2.** lamp removed; **3.** lights added; **4.** sheep's head turned white; **5.** light string added; **6.** mailbox became vertical; **7.** antlers removed; **8.** Santa riding sleigh backward—hope he doesn't lose his way!

In the Toy Department, *(page 96)* **1.** White pom-pom deleted; **2.** black toes turned brown; **3.** white tag removed; **4.** V-neck shirt became crewneck; **5.** tree tag upside-down; **6.** red Santa hat now green; **7.** cord missing; **8.** cart moved down.

■ **Ceramics Class,** *(page 100)* **1.** Scarf shortened; **2.** yellow trim turned red; **3.** eyebrows connected—Santa has a unibrow!; **4.** orange pom-pom turned blue; **5.** brown detail added; **6.** emblem became square; **7.** bow removed; **8.** cheeks reddened—snowman must be embarrassed.

■ **On the Antlers of a Dilemma,** *(page 101)* **1.** Stocking added—family expanded?; **2.** flame extinguished; **3.** red bow now blue; **4.** necklace missing; **5.** paw hiding; **6.** ring added; **7.** antler flipped right; **8.** white section turned black; **9.** white light added.

■ **Puzzling Packages,** *(pages 102–103)* **1.** Red tree removed; **2.** gold star added; **3.** holes in snowflake filled in; **4.** light green circle enlarged; **5.** candy cane flipped to right; **6.** berry bunch blossomed; **7.** gold tree grew; **8.** leaf trimmed.

■ **An Old-Fashioned Christmas,** *(page 104)* **1.** Clock detail enlarged; **2.** stocking lengthened—more room for treats!; **3.** popcorn string added; **4.** ornament removed; **5.** white ornament added; **6.** pants darkened; **7.** picture upside-down; **8.** gift added.

■ **The Light Fantastic,** *(page 105)* **1.** Light added in photo 1.

■ *Sale*-a-brate!, *(page 106)* **1.** Light fixture gone; **2.** stripe on balloon erased; **3.** blimp turned around—off to a different department?; **4.** red ornament turned green; **5.** bucket added; **6.** green ornament added; **7.** wood piece removed; **8.** arms now behind back.

■ Step Up to the Plate, *(page 107)* **1.** Bird flipped; **2.** green center turned white; **3.** fork became a spoon; **4.** red fruit missing—presumed eaten; **5.** white flower design added; **6.** candle moved to right; **7.** poinsettia leaf extended; **8.** place mat removed; **9.** red berries added.

■ Waterfront Light Show, *(page 111)* **1.** Antenna thicker; **2.** lights extended down; **3.** window filled in; **4.** reflection erased; **5.** white scarf turned brown; **6.** light added; **7.** spire moved left; **8.** trim removed.

■ Trial by Fire, *(pages 108–109)* **1.** Vent taller; **2.** figure removed; **3.** grout widened; **4.** log removed—fuel for the fire?; **5.** candle added; **6.** ornament deleted; **7.** moon facing left; **8.** ornament now white; **9.** branch pruned.

■ Gift Bagged, *(page 112)* **1.** Fireplace tool removed; **2.** circular stone became square; **3.** white tie now red; **4.** cap removed—too hot above the fireplace!; **5.** glasses taken off; **6.** red ribbon added; **7.** cracker end extended; **8.** gold ornament added.

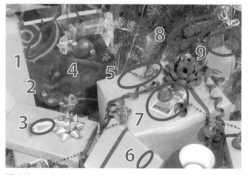

■ Wrap It Up, *(page 110)* **1.** Spiral added; **2.** gold ornament top removed; **3.** tree upside-down; **4.** star became circle; **5.** bell flipped; **6.** blue ribbon added; **7.** white border turned blue; **8.** branch extended; **9.** red bow turned green.

■ A Snowy Ride, *(page 113)* **1.** Lantern deleted in photo 2.

■ Holiday Village Stumper, *(page 114)* **1.** Time changed to 3:00; **2.** wreath missing; **3.** twig added; **4.** sign upside-down; **5.** barrier removed; **6.** light turned red; **7.** red hat became white; **8.** green block turned red; **9.** button missing.

■ One-Stop Shopping, *(page 118)* **1.** Moon design moved right; **2.** shopper went home—crowded holiday rush was too much!; **3.** bar removed; **4.** letter O became an A; **5.** red ornament added; **6.** white hat turned pink; **7.** arch became square; **8.** yellow light added.

■ Not a Creature Was Stirring . . . , *(page 115)* **1.** Stocking flipped to left; **2.** grout line removed; **3.** scarf lengthened; **4.** holly moved to center; **5.** red ornament turned green; **6.** grate bar removed; **7.** fireplace tool added; **8.** leaf enlarged.

■ Just Desserts, *(page 119)* **1.** Strawberry eaten; **2.** chocolate glob added; **3.** red ribbon extended; **4.** candle extinguished; **5.** ribbon removed; **6.** forks added—there's more than enough food; **7.** raspberry now chocolate-covered; **8.** red ribbon added.

■ All Spruced Up, *(pages 116–117)* **1.** Round handle became square; **2.** I became T on block; **3.** ribbon deleted; **4.** ornament lost; **5.** ornament added; **6.** glass taller; **7.** fork upside-down; **8.** tree chopped down; **9.** red napkin lighter.

■ *Zen* and Now, *(page 120)* **1.** Number 2 became a letter N in photo 4.

■ Let There Be Light, *(page 121)* **1.** Edge of roof missing; **2.** garland needs fixing; **3.** crossbar missing; **4.** light strand changed direction; **5.** triangular rooftop removed—heavy renovations!; **6.** garland extended; **7.** nutcracker upside-down; **8.** crossbar removed; **9.** lights extended downward.

■ Secret Santa, *(page 122)* **1.** Wall hanging extended; **2.** spiral missing; **3.** branch grew; **4.** U-neck now square; **5.** snowman and tree switched spots; **6.** blue ornament now green; **7.** shadow gone; **8.** figure deleted; **9.** flame added—another log thrown on fire?

■ Alpine High, *(page 123)* **1.** Snow covered path; **2.** ski lift moved left; **3.** shadow disappeared; **4.** another shadow gone; **5.** red helmet became green; **6.** head hiding under hood; **7.** blue marker added; **8.** red patches removed; **9.** mountain grew.

■ Chocolate Challenge, *(pages 124–125)* **1.** Red ornament turned blue; **2.** gold star added; **3.** red ribbon turned gold; **4.** orange section now green; **5.** chocolate drizzle extended; **6.** flame rose; **7.** light added; **8.** chocolate berry added.

■ Fire Drill, *(page 126)* **1.** Green ribbon turned white; **2.** silver ornament turned red; **3.** candy cane missing—presumed eaten; **4.** stripe made red; **5.** light added; **6.** 18 became 81; **7.** tooth grew in; **8.** hose nozzle added.

■ Alley Oops, *(page 127)* **1.** Figure taller; **2.** planter box deleted—tree planted?; **3.** dark line added; **4.** light turned off; **5.** tree grew; **6.** snowflake added; **7.** rabbit missing; **8.** light extended downward.

LEVEL 4

■ **Christmas Cluster,** *(page 131)* **1.** Walnut cluster added in photo 3.

■ **Noel, Noel,** *(page 128)* **1.** Red ball smaller; **2.** target moved to left; **3.** red leaf added; **4.** window filled in; **5.** blue patch erased; **6.** window replaced with door; **7.** leaf grew; **8.** opening in bell filled in; **9.** line in E extended; **10.** mouth erased.

■ **Group of Gifts,** *(page 129)* **1.** Star added; **2.** blue star appeared; **3.** heart deleted; **4.** tail of star erased; **5.** yellow ribbon added; **6.** wreath bigger; **7.** snowflake deleted; **8.** ribbon turned blue; **9.** outer heart gone; **10.** star disappeared.

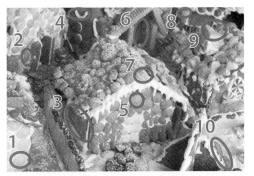

■ **Gingerbread Neighborhood,** *(page 132)* **1.** Yellow candy deleted; **2.** pink candy turned yellow; **3.** graham cracker wall eaten; **4.** smile became frown; **5.** blue candy turned white; **6.** pink wafer added; **7.** pink candy replaced green candy; **8.** yellow candy turned green; **9.** wafers and frosting added; **10.** green and red candies switched places.

■ **Snowed In,** *(page 130)* **1.** Hill of snow accumulated; **2.** chimney added; **3.** window bigger; **4.** front of house covered in snow—snowed in?; **5.** house became dark brown; **6.** small window added; **7.** tree appeared; **8.** windows filled in; **9.** chimney erased; **10.** little tree moved right.

■ **Cozy Kids,** *(page 133)* **1.** Arm of couch raised; **2.** books added; **3.** green stitches turned blue; **4.** red book taller; **5.** blue stitches now red; **6.** gift box became black; **7.** book turned green; **8.** bow deleted; **9.** afghan square all black; **10.** stripe deleted.

Lights of London, *(pages 134–135)* **1.** Lamppost taller; **2.** reflection of lights longer; **3.** star bigger; **4.** person left—too cold?; **5.** pole erased; **6.** light illuminated; **7.** column vanished; **8.** window filled in; **9.** reflection of lights disappeared; **10.** branch added.

■ Now, Dasher! Now, Dancer!, *(page 138)*
1. Black rectangle extended; **2.** arrow changed direction; **3.** red roof detail removed; **4.** LAKE erased from sign; **5.** deer head hiding in snow—he must be cold!; **6.** black hoof buried in snow, too; **7.** fish facing left; **8.** branch pruned; **9.** base enlarged; **10.** snow melted.

■ Doll-Making Workshop, *(page 136)* **1.** Red stripes added; **2.** board taller; **3.** red sleeve deleted; **4.** embroidery disappeared; **5.** scissors taken away; **6.** hat turned blue; **7.** stripes deleted; **8.** box turned red; **9.** hole in box lid filled in; **10.** label erased.

■ Perplexing Place Setting, *(page 139)* **1.** Holly berries gone in photo 1.

■ Interior Decorating, *(page 137)* **1.** Pillow became solid cream; **2.** curtain extended; **3.** gold cord deleted; **4.** candlestick vanished; **5.** fireplace taller; **6.** light burned out; **7.** ribbon ends cut off; **8.** candle taller; **9.** present added; **10.** pinecone appeared.

■ Mind the Store, *(page 140)* **1.** Red stripe turned green; **2.** birds switched places; **3.** gold pom-pom turned red; **4.** flower added; **5.** red flower appeared; **6.** red pom-pom added; **7.** another board appeared; **8.** ladder rung deleted—step carefully, Santa!; **9.** fur trim turned black; **10.** branch appeared.

See the Light, *(page 141)* 1. Window filled in; 2. lights burned out; 3. candy cane flipped other direction; 4. row of lights taken down; 5. door frame painted green; 6. shutter erased; 7. Santa removed; 8. circle completed; 9. stripe thinner; 10. Santa vanished.

The Christmas Story, *(pages 142–143)* 1. Ornament moved up and left; 2. ornament taken down; 3. string of beads added; 4. branch deleted; 5. loose curls cut; 6. holly sprigs erased; 7. button fell off; 8. hinge added; 9. bow removed; 10. cookie tin vanished—someone's hungry!

Nutcrackers Old and New, *(page 144)* 1. Feather enlarged; 2. white rope turned red; 3. red spot filled in with gold; 4. gold ball bigger; 5. white dot added; 6. button appeared; 7. shoe became U-shape; 8. ribbon cut off; 9. rope moved to other shoulder; 10. nose deleted.

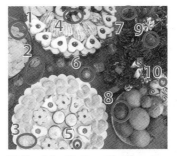

Cookie-Cutter Challenge, *(page 145)* 1. Potato chips added; 2. walnut moved down; 3. cookie flipped other direction; 4. horseshoe-shape cookie appeared; 5. chocolate center filled in; 6. ornament smaller; 7. branches added; 8. kiwi replaced by orange; 9. apple ornament bigger; 10. nut eaten.

Jingle Bell Jumble, *(page 146)* 1. Coil of ribbon deleted; 2. gold spiral added; 3. bell appeared; 4. ribbon turned red; 5. gold bead bigger; 6. cuff became solid white; 7. snowflake shape filled in; 8. ornament taken down; 9. belt buckle bigger; 10. red bead turned blue.

Skating Rink Riddler, *(page 147)* 1. Green sign became red EXIT sign; 2. skater gone—worn out?; 3. skater moved left; 4. silver line removed; 5. store sign erased; 6. lights turned off; 7. cone added; 8. object removed; 9. skater changed direction; 10. pink shirt turned yellow.

Ornamentally Yours, *(page 148)* **1.** Mouse ear smaller in photo 3.

Christmas Village, *(page 149)* **1.** Girl moved left; **2.** tree added; **3.** design upside-down; **4.** more snow appeared; **5.** hat turned blue; **6.** snow blew away; **7.** vertical trim added; **8.** window doubled in size; **9.** chimney taller and more ribbon added; **10.** lights turned off.

Tree Trimming Teaser, *(pages 150–151)* **1.** Ornament added; **2.** ribbon turned gold; **3.** crossbar added; **4.** pink ornament now blue; **5.** lights added; **6.** ribbon longer; **7.** confetti swept up; **8.** nose longer— has Santa been telling lies?; **9.** doll hand moved; **10.** gold pom-pom became silver ball.

Oh, Holy Night, *(page 152)* **1.** Lamppost moved right; **2.** bell deleted; **3.** gold light turned red; **4.** green light now blue; **5.** PEACE burned out; **6.** green star disappeared; **7.** bell and wreath switched places; **8.** lamppost appeared; **9.** another tree planted; **10.** NEW YEAR replaced with CHRISTMAS.

The Present Predicament, *(page 153)* **1.** Bow deleted; **2.** present moved left; **3.** mailbox flag erased; **4.** snowman vanished; **5.** ornament deleted; **6.** gift tag added—now we know who it's for!; **7.** ornament moved down and right; **8.** snowman's hat now blue; **9.** bow became blue; **10.** snowflake deleted.

Trays of Treats, *(page 154)* **1.** Center of cookie turned red; **2.** macadamia nut eaten; **3.** desserts switched places; **4.** walnut added; **5.** nut bigger; **6.** hazelnut added; **7.** red present moved up and right; **8.** leaf grew; **9.** walnut vanished; **10.** center of cookie filled in.

■ Poinsettia Puzzle, *(page 155)* **1.** Cluster of leaves turned white in photo 6.

■ No Time Like the Present . . . , *(pages 158–159)* **1.** Branch appeared; **2.** bow deleted; **3.** star gone; **4.** ribbon turned green; **5.** gold ornament now red; **6.** ribbon removed; **7.** star deleted; **8.** branch fuller; **9.** silver gift box appeared; **10.** handle of bag turned red.

■ Window-Shopping Wonderland, *(page 156)* **1.** Lights extended; **2.** wreath and snowflake switched spots; **3.** beam removed; **4.** yellow and green windows switched; **5.** wreath gone; **6.** beam extended; **7.** door panels removed; **8.** decoration moved up and left; **9.** garland deleted; **10.** red bow turned green.

■ Snowy Street Scene, *(page 160)* **1.** Bar added; **2.** cord deleted; **3.** snowflake moved right; **4.** pipe angled to right; **5.** doorknob on other side; **6.** someone took out the garbage; **7.** person went home; **8.** door decorations switched places; **9.** bar removed; **10.** house number 33 now number 30.

■ Christmas Eve Challenge, *(page 157)* **1.** Stocking bigger; **2.** gold trim added; **3.** candle shorter—must have been burning for a long time; **4.** stocking moved left; **5.** hurricane added; **6.** white window frame deleted; **7.** side of box turned white; **8.** ornament deleted; **9.** white ornament turned red; **10.** wrapping paper now solid red.

■ Family Gathering, *(page 161)* **1.** Sleeve now solid green; **2.** tie turned solid purple; **3.** ribbon widened; **4.** spine of book now yellow; **5.** group of books removed—someone catching up on their reading?; **6.** ribbon erased; **7.** necklace now black; **8.** bow bigger; **9.** buttons turned black; **10.** pant leg longer.

ANSWERS

■ Beads, Bags, and Baubles, *(page 162)*
1. Ornament center turned pink; **2.** bead now white; **3.** flame grew; **4.** center of snowflake deleted; **5.** bell disappeared; **6.** gold rope now a green row of beads; **7.** Santa's belt missing; **8.** ornament taken down; **9.** facial hair grew; **10.** ornament taken away.

■ Nativity Activity, *(page 163)* **1.** Another sheep appeared in photo 2.

■ Transformed Table, *(pages 164–165)*
1. Peppercorns added; **2.** knife moved up; **3.** gold star bigger; **4.** mustache grew; **5.** mustache shaved off; **6.** rocking horse deleted; **7.** fork taken away; **8.** small bottle appeared; **9.** cluster of confetti added; **10.** knife removed.

■ So Many Snowmen and Santas . . . , *(page 166)* **1.** Tree became solid green; **2.** scarf turned solid red; **3.** purple ornament appeared; **4.** mustache turned black; **5.** red nose became white; **6.** hat bigger; **7.** eyes deleted; **8.** eyes bigger; **9.** scarf removed; **10.** star vanished.

■ Winterlude Challenge, *(page 167)* **1.** White tower deleted; **2.** arch squared off; **3.** window added; **4.** pole deleted; **5.** white awning turned green; **6.** person went home—tired of waiting in line?; **7.** person added; **8.** post taller; **9.** yellow pole turned green; **10.** roofline evened out.

■ Snow-covered Cabins, *(page 168)* **1.** Light burned out; **2.** pole erased; **3.** pole thicker; **4.** light turned on—someone must have come home; **5.** windows filled in; **6.** snow added; **7.** snow accumulated on mound; **8.** vertical beam put up; **9.** horizontal beam added; **10.** another porch appeared.